Vietnamese

Vietnamese

Emily Nguyen

Published in 2014 by
New Holland Publishers
London • Sydney • Cape Town • Auckland

The Chandlery Unit 114, 50 Westminster Bridge Road, London, SE1 7QY UK
1/66 Gibbes Street, Chatswood, NSW 2067, Australia
Wembley Square First Floor, Solan Road Gardens, Cape Town 8001, South Africa
218 Lake Road, Northcote, Auckland, New Zealand

www.newhollandpublishers.com

A catalogue record of this book is available at the British Library and the
National Library of Australia.

ISBN: 9781742575513

Managing Director: Fiona Schultz
Design: Linda Gregor
Editor: Emily Carryer
Production Director: Olga Dementiev
Printer: Toppan Leefung Printing Ltd (China)

10 9 8 7 6 5 4 3 2 1

Follow New Holland Publishers on
Facebook: www.facebook.com/NewHollandPublishers

Contents

Vietnamese
Simply Delicious

Introduction

The land and its people

FOOD FOR ALL MOODS

On a cold, blustery morning in a narrow, muddied, unsealed, suburban street in Hanoi, the capital of Vietnam, buyers and sellers of vegetables, fruit and flowers and food hawkers huddled under canvas awnings shading shadowy shops. While it was hot in the country's south, here, in the north, we sheltered from pelting rain. Suddenly one of the shopkeepers ignited a huge wad of newspapers. Tossing sections towards the road, she created a mini-inferno.

I wondered if she had gone mad, a modern-day victim of more than 2,000 years in which war-torn Vietnam had struggled to expel foreign demons and cope with its own violent rebellions. My young interpreter, Mai, grasped my hand, reassuring me that 'The seller fans the fire to highlight her vegetables' – a simple but effective marketing technique.

I was in Hanoi to become, I believe, the first western woman to take a professional crash course in tertiary cooking with Madame Do Minh Thu at the Caoson College of Learning, one of one of Hanoi's five university campuses. Mai, and her fellow students Tek and Hanh, drove me to the course every day as a motorbike pillion-passenger, weaving expertly through the city's insane traffic.

Mai and Tek bought in large quantities from the flame-thrower and other vendors. Later, at Mai's family's narrow, three-storey home, designed to give maximum space to the vegetable garden (in the style of many city houses), the girls prepared a host of dishes while squatting on the kitchen floor. Many Vietnamese kitchens are tiny, with negligible bench space, a reason why many Vietnamese cook and eat out on the streets. Three invisible food gods presided over the nervous chefs, who had both learned to cook from their mothers.

Until recently, all Vietnamese girls were expected to prove their culinary skills to a future husband's family before marriage, which they still do in some villages. Mai and Tet would pass these tests with flying colours.

A staple of Vietnam is long-grain rice steamed until fluffy in a rice cooker (a more important appliance in Vietnam than a refrigerator). Sticky or glutinous rice is usually reserved for desserts and special festival food but is often spiced and served for breakfast, wrapped in banana leaves. The world's biggest exporter of rice, next to America and Thailand, Vietnam has dozens of varieties of rice. Rice (cooked unwashed without salt) appears as rice flour, food-wrapping paper, powder, noodles, vermicelli, wine and vinegar.

Professional cooking courses are relatively new to Vietnam. In recent years visitors have taken short, rather westernised courses in the 1901-built grand Metropole Hotel in Hanoi, as well as in other hotels and restaurants in Hanoi and Saigon. You need a course of at least three days to explore the northern and southern Vietnamese cooking styles, which are both very different. A distinctive central region cuisine was developed in the former imperial courts of Hue and in the French-influenced old port of Hoi An.

Dominated by China from 200 BC, Vietnam inherited from the Chinese metal ploughs, irrigation systems, beasts of burden, chopsticks, Buddhism (hence vegetarianism), many recipes, table manners and, most importantly, rice cultivation. Cattle were brought to Vietnam by 10th century Mongol herdsman. Hanoi gave birth to the wonderful beef noodle soup pho (pronounced 'fur'), which is Vietnam's national dish.

Thai traditions filtered into Vietnam at about the time the Portuguese missionaries introduced spices and Christianity to Thailand in the 14th century AD. Coffee and tea came to Vietnam via Cambodia. Coffee plants now cover Vietnam's countryside which was devastated by bomb blasts during the Vietnam War. The Vietnamese are also fond of curries.

The French occupied Vietnam from 1859 to 1954, and left their imprint on Vietnamese cuisine. The French influence ranges from the introduction of produce such as wine, avocados, tomatoes, asparagus, sweetcorn, baguettes, pâté, salads, pastries, café au lait, cakes and ice cream, as well as the cooking method of sautéing.

The result of all these cultural influences is a rich array of tastes and traditions. Vietnamese food is not as spicy as Thai but is crisper. Soy sauce is not used much, unlike in China. Having eaten my way from Hanoi to Ho Chi Minh City, I believe Vietnamese cuisine to be the most exciting on earth. The secret is in nuoc cham, a pungent fish sauce. Nuoc cham is to the Vietnamese what soy is to the Chinese and Japanese, shrimp paste to the Indonesians and nam prik (chilli sauce) is to the Thais. Fermented from anchovies, bottled nuoc cham is used instead of salt and combines well with all meats and fish. Add lime juice, garlic, fresh, seeded red chilli, and sugar and vinegar to taste, and it becomes Vietnam's favourite dipping sauce, also known as nuoc cham, found on every table.

IS THERE AN 'S' IN VIETNAM?

'S' is the shape of the country of Vietnam, which has a population of more than 70 million people, including 54 different ethnic groups.

You can picture Vietnam as a street vendor with his head raised, his thin spine curved under the heavy burden of a bamboo pole yoke (don ganh) balanced on his frail shoulders with each end of the bamboo pole holding a big basket containing anything from bananas to bricks. His knees are bent. In the far south, including the Mekong Delta, the map resembles a foot, poised ready to repel adversaries into the Gulf of Thailand.

The S-shape also represents the national highway which winds from north to south for about 1,600 km along the Indochinese Peninsula in an area a bit bigger than the 'boot' of the south of Italy. The national highway is a paradoxically both a good and bad way to traverse Vietnam. In seasons of monsoons and typhoons the road is subject to flooding and mudslides and is pot-holed and sometimes terrifying. Through bus windows, one sees an endless lake of rice paddies punctuated by the conical hats of women working. Running past shark-toothed mountains, the bus affords views of the Gulf of Tonkin and the South China Sea. There is a train at night but its passengers miss the stunning beauty of the countryside.

The Vietnamese countryside is dotted with waterfalls, rain forests, lagoons, groves of coconut palms and other tropical fruit trees. Cattle, water buffalo and goats graze in the pastures. There is an intriguing mixture of prosperous and depressed towns (curiously, all advertising photocopying facilities) and an increasing number of resorts.

The climate in Vietnam is varied, from cold in winter to a hot dry summer in the north, to southern humidity. The central mountains, where the French built hill stations, provide respite from the summer heat.

Much of Vietnam is sub-tropical and hence there is an astonishing variety of fresh produce. In Dalat, Vietnam's honeymoon capital, the terraced hills are so abundant with vegetables and fruits that many residents are vegetarians. Ho Chi Minh City is lavishly supplied with fresh daily produce, including tea and coffee from surrounding plantations. Local wineries are developing in the lowlands extending from the South China Sea where the climate favours grapes.

Vietnam's 3,260 kilometres of coastline yields gleaming fish and seafood. Fish are also harvested from the Red, Perfume and Mekong Rivers, as well as in countless canals and ponds.

THE PEOPLE

Whether bent in the fields (80 per cent of people toil in agriculture), spinning silk, making lacquerware, copying famous artworks of European masters, manning stalls, endlessly serving food, hobbling along streets burdened by their don ganh yokes, or working in offices, the Vietnamese are friendly and hospitable. They don't demonstrate any resentment towards nationalities with whom they have previously been at war. Visitors need only be prepared for the amusing attention from competing owners of pho shops seeking custom and from the bargaining drivers of cyclos (cycle-cabs for one or two passengers), eager for passengers.

Although from a mix of Asian religions, Christianity, and Islam (a minority only), all Vietnamese people celebrate the seven-day Tet festival (Vietnamese New Year) with gusto, eating special foods such as sticky rice, yellow beans and spiced pig fat boiled for six hours in banana leaves. Sweetmeats, dried, sugar and salted fruits are sold en masse. Tet occurs in the lunar calendar in late January or early February. Wandering Souls' Day on the 15th day of the seventh month is the second largest festival in Vietnam. Gifts, mainly fruits, are taken to pagodas and sweets to houses as tributes to the souls of the dead.

Food is paramount in the Mid-Autumn festival on the 15th day of the eighth lunar month; a festival filled with bright, noisy night processions. A January rice-cooking festival in Hanoi also enlivens the lunar calendar.

Vietnam is a bountiful paradise where many live in poverty, yet its proud people don't eat to live. They live to eat.

Daily food in Vietnam

LE PETIT DEJEUNER

Just before sunrise in Hanoi's old quarter, courting couples called it a day after conquering the night with their screaming motorcycles. Apart from crowding into Internet cafes or flirting over pho, motorcycling seems to be the most popular entertainment for young people. No girls were out wearing ao dai, their traditional costume of long white pants and a modest thigh-length, wrist-touching top, along with coolie hats and gloves (to keep their hands untanned).

Street sweepers shuffled slowly. Light filtered through an avenue of leafy trees. An old woman painstakingly arranged eggs in the baskets of her doh ganh; white in one basket, brown in the other. Shopkeepers and residents gradually emerged to peruse hawkers' vegetables, fruit, meat and fish. Flower vendors offered bright blooms from the baskets of their bicycles. One soup seller's business was busy with manicurists and pedicurists sitting on small plastic stools. Between attending to their female clients, the beauticians spooned up chao (rice porridge) or soup, using chopsticks to fish for their noodles.

An aged street barber was massaging the neck of his disabled son who was sitting in a primitive wheelchair. A pre-World War II Citroen halted by a large pottery shop where salesgirls were eating pho with salad. A woman offered me sticky rice in banana-leaf parcels in French – just to taste, no charge unless I liked it. But I'd had already had my pho fix. In plush hotels, French continental breakfast rolls, croissants and pastries were baking. In the fields, men were drinking tea together and eating rice with fish sauce.

Hanoi's seven million people begin every day like this. Their repasts are on the move as they are everywhere in Vietnam. Baguette bikes tow mobile stalls from dawn until dark.

Children have a choice of either morning or afternoon sessions at school. Some children breakfast at home but are more likely to eat market food with a parent before school starts at 7.30 am. The second session begins after a lunch at home or at the market.

Although coffee aficionados might disagree, Vietnamese coffee, brewed strong and slowly, is delicious. It is always consumed at breakfast and after dinner, with milk or cream and sugar. Tea is drunk everywhere in Vietnam and its serving is elevated to an art form as in China, although tea, I was warned, is far too strong for females in the morning. While black tea is cheap, green tea is expensive. In the central mountains, artichoke tea is popular.

In Dalat, inhabitants eat chao, but it is quite unlike the bland rice porridge eaten elsewhere in Vietnam. Dalat chao is also favoured in the evening as warming fuel for those in the cool mountainous terrain. This thick gruel is pork broth based, with meat or fish chunks, garlic and chilli oil added, and topped with coriander, bean sprouts and black pepper. It makes a filling dinner. In southern Dalat one morning, I grabbed a hot melt-in-the-mouth, pâté-stuffed puff-pastry from a patisserie and became instantly hooked on another specialty of this area.

In the Mekong Delta's Cai Rang and on Phu Quoc, one of several islands (and Vietnam's most famous source of nuoc cham), floating marketeers feed early risers. Each fragile vessel carries a speciality – fruits, vegetables, fish, pork, rice, noodles, baguettes, tea, coffee and even breakfast beer.

Starting from Ninh Binh town, my friend and I glided in a traditional rowboat through Tam Coc (the name means 'three caves') along the Ngo Dong River. This river supplies a canal system for rice irrigation. Its spectacular rock formations were like those in Halong Bay and were reminiscent of China's Guilin and Yangzhou. The sole western visitors, other than holidaying French people, we were assailed in French by boat folk. These boat vendors would row or pole back a long way to the port if they didn't have pho, fish, water, beer, fruit, embroidered napery, hats, film, or even rice hooch, such is their enthusiasm.

My friend became addicted to Vietnamese smoothies – not the same as western thick-shakes. Melting ice is blended with sweetened condensed milk, a mint sprig, lime or lemon juice, plus any fruit or, for savoury smoothies, avocado, tomato or pumpkin, or any combination of these, garnished with coriander. Created for western budget-backpackers, smoothies have been happily adopted by busy, young Vietnamese as healthy breakfast starters and as lunchtime coolers.

DEJEUNER – AH, LUNCH

Markets in cities, towns, villages and on fishing waterfronts are abuzz after first light in Vietnam. Those who can go home for lunch, do, but still the street eateries, cafes, restaurants and markets are crammed with people.

Westerners would recognise much Vietnamese lunch fare as snack food or appetisers: spring rolls and rice paper rolls, cold or hot, and other tasty tidbits (see the Appetisers section). On sale for lunch in Vietnam are noodles, rice cakes, baguettes, grilled meats, seafood, pho and plain steamed rice with fish sauce. People tend to eat at any time of the day. Desserts are something snacked on, rather than eaten as part of a main meal.

From 11 am to noon and onward, Vietnam lunches. At home, women usually cook, while professional cooks and chefs are mostly men. A typical home meal would be rice with soup plus two to three other dishes, one a salad, or sautéed, fried or boiled vegetables. Weekend, and particularly Sunday, lunches are leisurely for those families not working then, who, if they can afford it, add an extra dish or two.

Fish or meat is not usually eaten daily because meat, particularly beef, is more expensive than vegetables. Sheep are not bred in Vietnam. Edible leaves are used to garnish and wrap food in neat packets. You need to be wary of eating salads in Vietnam, as the raw vegetables may have been washed in contaminated water. Frequently combined with meat, poultry or fish, Vietnamese salads are delicious and easy to prepare in your own kitchen (see Salads section). Monosodium glutamate is used in many Vietnamese dishes to enhance the flavour. As some people are allergic to MSG, it has been left out of the authentic recipes which follow.

Utensils for Vietnamese cooking are simple: one pot for rice, one for slow cooking, the essential mortar and pestle (or a blender or food processor), and a couple of pans. A wok is unnecessary but helpful. Some Vietnamese use a coolie-hat-shaped pan, similar to a wok. You will need also both large and small sharp knives, an optional cleaver for chopping poultry, a chopping board, chopsticks, bowls with saucers, small bowls for sauces, serving dishes with spoons and tiny cups for tea.

LE DINER – HOME AT LAST

Dinner is time for hard-working Vietnamese parents to be reunited with their children and elderly relatives. Dinner dishes are similar to home-prepared lunches, centred around the rice bowl and all served simultaneously with soup. Dinner could comprise up to eight dishes on special occasions. Fruit is usually served for dessert.

Before eating, guests in the north should wait until the oldest host is seated and until he or she places something in their bowl. Southerners are more casual. It is customary to leave the last tasty morsel in a serving bowl to be offered to the host. He or she will then offer it back to the guest. Some leftovers should remain in the individual bowls to indicate the family has been generous. But do not leave rice in your bowl. A belief exists that if precious rice, the staple, is wasted on earth, a departed soul could be denied basic sustenance in the other world.

In the countryside, cooking is usually done outdoors over a coal brazier. With no refrigeration, shopping at the market may be done twice daily. Small city kitchens may have only two gas or electric hotplates. Most don't have ovens – hence the method of slow pot-cooking. Other Vietnamese cooking methods include sautéing, stir- and deep-frying, boiling and grilling over a brazier. Vietnamese use a garlic-infused oil for frying. To prepare this, heat peanut oil but do not boil and then remove it from the burner, and add crushed garlic. Kept in a jar, garlic oil lasts about a week and is brushed on barbecued meat or fish, noodles, bread and vegetables. The garnishing and decoration of Vietnamese dishes is as important as the flavour and freshness of the ingredients.

Typical drinks include fruit and sugarcane juices, and fizzy soft drinks similar to western ones. Worth a try is non-fizzy bird's nest canned drink. Coconut milk is drunk through straws from punctured fresh coconuts. Few women drink alcohol. Men will imbibe light, refreshing beer with a meal out but most alcohol is consumed at home where ice cubes are often added to cool the beer! Wine, introduced by the French, is an acceptable accompaniment to Vietnamese food which is only as fiery as the chilli sauce or fresh, chopped chilli added by the diner. Moonshine is made from fermented sticky rice, husks, water and yeast. It was once only the tipple of a minority ethnic group, the mountain people, at celebrations but is now more popular in cities. It is cheap and readily available. Depending on where it was made and how long it has been fermented, the intensity of Vietnamese moonshine varies from bland to knock-out! (You can use vodka as a substitute aperitif at home.) As in Korea and China, 'snake wine' comes with the viper in the bottle. This liquor is very strong so beware.

EATING OUT IN VIETNAM

In Vietnam, pho houses and markets are must-sees. Markets can be smelly but their overwhelming flower perfumes are glorious. Street food is quite safe if the food is served hot. Noodle-soup stallholders bang together bamboo sections or pieces of metal to advertise their presence. You'll eat cheaply and well in or in front of a simple shop. There is no menu, you just point.

Simple eating establishments are called com (meaning rice). These are family-run, no-frills places. Some display picture menus if the com is a shop rather than a stall. Otherwise, eat in the street – perfect for people-watching.

Eager to try Hue's legendary seafood-stuffed crêpes, I wandered into a com. There was no menu but the place had both indoor and street seating. The intelligent old father was deaf and mute, so I drew a primitive picture. He rushed to his wife and daughter in the miniscule backyard and returned with a selection of canned drinks in his hands. I chose light beer. Soon, I was served by the women who then awaited my appraisal of the crêpes. 'Magnifique', I attested honestly.

Dog, cat, snake, field mice and rats, and embryo ducks from eggs are served in certain restaurants (though these recipes are not included).

Many shop or stalls sell desserts, cakes and sweetmeats. Pancake outlets serve savoury and sweet pancakes but differ from western pancake parlours. Waterfront restaurants, both indoor and out, abound in river and sea ports. Upmarket restaurants are found in major Vietnamese cities. Waiters may not speak English but a translated menu will give the number of the dish. Vietnamese music or European classical, mainly French composers, provide a soothing background. In international hotels, the ambience will be French-style with neatly laid tables, good service and Vietnamese/French/English menus. You should visit a hotel like the legendary Rex in Saigon for a drink, a rooftop view or elegant environment, even if you can't afford to dine there. More and more grand French mansions are being restored as high-class restaurants.

Even if you never visit Vietnam, I hope you can gain a understanding of this scenically sensational country and its warm people through its delicate yet hearty cuisine, which boasts more than 5,000 dishes. Hue's 19th century emperor Tu Duc demanded 50 dishes in each single meal, never to be served more than twice in the same year. Imperial chefs created more than 2,000 dishes during his reign.

Appetisers & snacks

Appetisers and snacks
Roll on a wrap

'It's a wrap,' says a film director when a movie scene is finally finished to satisfaction. But a 'wrap' in a Vietnamese kitchen, street market and or hawker stall means a super snack. At home, a 'wrap' can signify the beginning of a meal or party – cocktail, luncheon or dinner – as so many Vietnamese appetisers come in these tasty parcels.

Wraps may be deep- or shallow-fried, steamed or packed in fresh edible leaves – banana, lettuce, spinach, or cabbage – to be served cool. Wraps are delectable dollops of mixed ingredients folded in rice paper, crêpes, thicker pancakes or omelettes.

Spring rolls are served with nuoc cham dipping sauce (see page 39). As China has exerted great influence on Vietnamese food, soy sauce is often an ingredient in wraps too. Soy sauce is likely to be on Vietnamese tables as a dipping sauce too and many westerners prefer it to fish sauce. Use Vietnamese, Thai, Japanese or Chinese soy sauce as American-made is too salty. Finely sliced, small, seeded red chillies are also a good spring roll accompaniment.

White Sauce

45 g (1½ oz) butter
3 shallots, chopped
3 tablespoons plain flour
200 ml (7 fl oz) full-fat milk
salt and black pepper

Heat the butter in a saucepan, then fry the shallots for 5 minutes. Stir in the flour and cook for 2 minutes, stirring. Stir in the milk and cook for 20 minutes, stirring often.

Hue Stuffed Pancakes

oil for frying

55 g (2 oz) flour seasoned with salt and
pepper

2 eggs, beaten

extra oil for deep frying

BATTER

85 g (2¾ oz) rice flour

½ cup coconut milk

3 eggs, beaten

pinch salt

FILLING

½ tablespoon ginger root, peeled and
chopped

1 clove garlic, chopped

1 tablespoon soy sauce

125 ml (4 oz) white sauce (see page 33)

145 g (5 oz) crab meat

85 g (3 oz) mushrooms, chopped

30 g (1 oz) spring onions, chopped

30 g (1 oz) bean sprouts

salt and pepper

TO SERVE

lettuce leaves

coriander leaves, chopped

nuoc cham dipping sauce

1 red chilli, seeded and finely sliced

To make batter, combine, rice flour, coconut milk, eggs and salt. Heat some oil in a
20 cm (8 in) pan (preferably non-stick) add enough batter to coat base. Cook for 2
minutes. Repeat with remaining batter. Put all pancakes aside.

To make filling, blend ginger, garlic, soy and white sauce. Add crab meat,
mushrooms, spring onions, and bean sprouts and season to taste. Place a spoonful of
the mixture on to each pancake. Tuck in ends and roll up so mixture doesn't escape.

Carefully roll each pancake in seasoned flour then in beaten egg. Deep-fry until
golden. Serve on lettuce leaves, sprinkled with chopped coriander, accompanied by
nuoc cham.

For variation, use thinly rolled puff pastry instead of pancakes. Pancakes can also be filled
and served without deep-frying.

PRAWN CREPES

255 g (9 oz) rice flour
1 teaspoon salt
1½ teaspoons sugar
250 ml (9 fl oz) coconut milk
250 ml (9 fl oz) water
½ teaspoon ground turmeric
200 g (7 oz) king prawns, shelled
200 g (7 oz) bean shoots

100 g (3½ oz)pork fillet or chicken
1 onion, sliced
peanut oil (for frying)
nuoc cham dipping sauce

TO GARNISH

Vietnamese mint leaves
lettuce leaves

Mix together rice flour, salt, sugar, coconut milk, water and turmeric until the batter is smooth. Set aside.

Wash and dry prawns and chop roughly. Wash bean shoots and set aside.

Dice the pork or chicken.

Heat a large frying pan and pour in a little oil. Add pork, onion and prawns, and cook, stirring constantly, until prawns change colour and pork is cooked through.

Pour enough batter over mixture to cover ingredients, top with some bean shoots and cover pan with a lid. Cook for 2 minutes until crisp. Turn over and cook the other side until golden.

To serve: Place a Vietnamese mint leaf on a piece of the crêpe. Enclose in a lettuce leaf and drizzle nuoc cham over. Serve immediately.

Nuoc Cham Dipping Sauce

125 g (4 oz) golden caster sugar
1 cup hot water
½ cup Vietnamese fish sauce
1 tablespoon white rice vinegar
75 ml (2¼ oz) lime juice
2–4 small red or green chillies, finely chopped
3–5 large garlic cloves, finely chopped

Put the sugar in a bowl and pour the hot water over it, stirring until it is completely dissolved. Add all the other ingredients, stir well and allow to cool to room temperature.

This dipping sauce can be kept in an airtight container in the refrigerator for up to 7 days.

Madame Thu's Steamed Egg Roll

15 g (½ oz) dried wood ear mushrooms

2 duck eggs

rice wine or dry sherry

oil or pork fat for frying

2 cups water

1 banana leaf or muslin

200 g (7 oz) pork mince

1 teaspoon sesame seeds

2 cloves garlic, minced

2 pimientos or seeded red chillies, finely chopped

2 dessertspoons sugar

2 dessertspoons fish sauce

pinch black pepper

15 g (½ oz) field mushrooms

1 piece hot spicy cooked sausage, about 17.5 cm (7 inches)

length of string

nuoc cham dipping sauce

TO GARNISH

slices of cucumber, tomatoes, parboiled cauliflower florets and fresh parsley sprigs

Soak dried mushrooms in hot water for about 30 minutes until soft. Meanwhile, separate eggs into 2 bowls; whites in one, yolks in the other. Beat both, adding a little wine to the whites to reduce the eggy odor and a little to the yolks to make a medium thick consistency.

Season a pan with a little pork fat or oil, add some pork to flavour pan. Stir-fry over medium heat, then remove. Add egg white mixture to pan and, when firm, remove pancake form and place on a plate. Re-season pan with more pork fat or oil, then pour off excess oil and add beaten yolk and wine mixture.

Heat on a lower heat. When bubbles form on top of egg, turn off heat and place omelette on another plate. Boil 2 cups water, slip banana leaf in to clean and soften. Strain and place leaf or moistened muslin on a board.

Mix pork with sesame seeds, garlic, pimiento or chilli, sugar, fish sauce and pepper to taste. Remove stalks from dried mushrooms and discard. Add fresh mushrooms and pound until thin. Heat quickly in pan. Remove.

Place yolk omelette on a board. Spread one quarter raw pork mix over a spatula.

Top with mushrooms. Add another layer each of pork and mushrooms, place egg white circle on top then add another pork layer. Carefully press with oiled rolling pin, add single sausage and trim. Gently roll and fill in roll end with pork.

Place roll on banana leaf or muslin, tuck in ends and bind with string to hold shape. Steam in a double boiler for about 17 minutes. Remove and cool then refrigerate until cold.

Arrange half-moon shapes of cucumber around the edge of a serving plate then, inside the circle of cucumber, arrange tomato slices in a heart shape. Remove leaf or muslin from cold roll, slice to 1 cm (½ in) thickness and arrange in middle of the plate. Top with parsley sprigs.

These hors d'oeuvres are intended for a Valentine's Day party. Serve with nuoc cham dipping sauce.

Spring Rolls

20 g (⅔ oz) vermicelli (green bean thread)

3 tablespoons vegetable oil

3 cloves garlic, finely chopped

310 g (11 oz) minced chicken
   (or half crab meat, half pork)

¼ cabbage, cut into fine strips

1 carrot, cut into thin strips

2 spring onions, finely chopped

½ teaspoon salt

1 teaspoon sugar

½ teaspoon white pepper

1 tablespoon oyster sauce

20–25 rice-paper wrappers

1 egg, beaten

extra oil for deep frying

TO SERVE

lettuce and mint leaves

nuoc cham dipping sauce

Soak vermicelli for 5 minutes in hot water until soft. Drain, cut into 5 cm (2 in) lengths and reserve.

Heat 3 tablespoons oil in wok or pan. Add garlic and chicken (or crab and pork) and cook about 8 minutes, stirring so ingredients don't stick to pan. Add cabbage, carrot, spring onions and vermicelli and cook on high heat for 3 minutes or until vegetables soften.

Turn off heat, add salt, sugar, pepper and oyster sauce. Stir to mix well. When mixture is cool, brush each side of the rice wrappers with water or they will dry and break. Place 1 tablespoon of the mixture into each wrapper, turn sides in first, roll and seal each with beaten egg. Refrigerate until needed.

Heat extra oil in wok or pan. Deep-fry rolls until golden. Serve on lettuce leaves garnished with lettuce and mint and serve with bottled sweet chilli sauce or nuoc cham dipping sauce.

Rice Paper Wrappers

Makes about 20

85 g (3 oz) rice flour
3 cups water
salt to taste
oil

Make batter with flour, water and salt. Three-quarter fill the base of a double boiler with water and stretch a piece of muslin or cheesecloth firmly over the boiler's top and bind securely with string.

Bring water to boil. Brush fabric with oil and pour a little batter on, using a swirling motion with a spoon to spread it into a circle. Cover with a lid and leave a minute or so until firm. Carefully lift the wrapper with a spatula and set aside. Repeat until all batter is used. Wrappers can be stuffed with pre-cooked filling and served cold or filled and deep fried.

After making rice paper wrappers or opening a bought packet, dip the wrappers in water to soften and cover with a damp tea towel to retain moisture.

Vietnamese Herb Salad Rolls With Homemade Peanut Sauce

Makes 20

55 g (2 oz) cellophane noodles

3 tablespoons rice vinegar

1 tablespoon fish sauce

4 tablespoons roasted peanuts, crushed

12 large prawns, shelled, deveined, cooked and finely chopped

20 Thai basil leaves, finely sliced

10 Asian mint leaves, finely sliced

¼ cup coriander leaves, finely chopped

4 leaves of Chinese cabbage or bok choy, finely shredded

2 cabbage leaves, finely shredded

5 spring onions, julienned

1 medium carrot, grated

12–16 rice paper wrappers (20 cm/ 8 in)

PEANUT SAUCE

2 tablespoons peanut oil

5 cloves garlic, minced

½ small red chilli, minced

5 tablespoons peanut butter

1½ tablespoons tomato paste

3 tablespoons hoisin sauce

1 teaspoon sugar

1 teaspoon fish sauce

¾ cup water

¼ cup peanuts (crushed)

Soak the cellophane noodles in a bowl full of hot water for 5–10 minutes or until tender. Drain immediately and rinse with cold water (to halt the cooking time). Cut noodles, with scissors, to about 6 cm (2½ in) and toss with vinegar, fish sauce, crushed peanuts and prawns.

In a large bowl, mix together herbs, cabbage leaves (both sorts), spring onions, noodle mixture and grated carrot and toss thoroughly.

Working with 1 wrapper at a time, soak rice wrapper in warm water for 30 seconds and lie it on a flat surface. On each wrapper, place a small quantity of the mixed vegetable/noodle filling. Roll up tightly, folding the sides in to enclose the filling. Continue rolling and folding until all ingredients are used.

To make peanut sauce, heat oil and sauté garlic and minced chilli until softened (about 2 minutes), then add all remaining ingredients and whisk over moderate heat. Bring to the boil and simmer until thickened slightly (about 3 minutes).

To serve, slice each roll on the diagonal, then rest one half over the other. Serve the sauce separately in a small pot for dipping.

As these wrappers do fry successfully, you may like to serve half of them fresh and half of them deep-fried.

SHRIMP BALLS

3 drops rice wine or dry sherry

salt and black pepper, to taste

1 teaspoon sugar

55 g (2 oz) pork fat, minced

225 g (8 oz) shrimp or shelled prawns

1 dessertspoon finely ground peppercorns

1 small brown onion, finely chopped

225 g (8 oz) pork mince

1 dessertspoon fresh dill or parsley,
  chopped

1 small red chilli, seeded
  and finely chopped (optional)

1 chicken stock cube

handful breadcrumbs

1 egg, beaten

vegetable oil for deep-frying and handling

TO GARNISH

lettuce leaves, fresh coriander leaves
  and pared carrot strips

Combine drops of wine, pork fat, black pepper, sugar and a little salt in a bowl. Sit bowl in another bowl of hot water to melt the fat.

Chop shrimps or prawns very finely until mushy. Place in bowl. Add peppercorns and a little extra salt and pepper.

Fry onion until transparent, drain oil and add onion to pork mince. Combine, add shrimps and dill or parsley and/or optional chilli with shrimps and pork fat.

Crush stock cube finely and mix with breadcrumbs. Work some oil into your hands, form walnut-sized balls from the shrimp mix and dip each ball in beaten egg and then in breadcrumbs mix. Deep-fry in oil in a wok or pan until golden. Drain on kitchen paper and serve on a plate layered with lettuce. Top with coriander leaves and strips of pared carrot.

Seafood Sugarcane Skewers

1½ cups shrimps, or prawn or
  crab meat, minced
black pepper to taste
1 clove garlic, crushed
½ teaspoon fish sauce
1½ teaspoons sugar
1½ tablespoons vegetable oil
8 sticks sugarcane, 10 cm (4 in) long

TO SERVE
lettuce leaves and coriander sprigs
mint
1 red chilli, seeded and finely sliced
1 lime, sliced into 8 wedges
1 cup sweet and sour sauce

Combine seafood with pepper, garlic, fish sauce and sugar. Pound or blend until combined and refrigerate, covered, for about 8 hours.

Oil your hands, divide seafood paste into 8 and mould each portion smoothly around the centre of each sugarcane stick.

Grill or barbecue over medium heat until golden and crisp, or bake in a moderate oven for 15–20 minutes. Place on serving plates with lettuce, mint, coriander sprigs, slices of chilli and lime slices attractively arranged. Serve with sweet and sour sauce.

Prawns in Caramel

Serves 4

455 g (15½ oz) raw prawns
5 spring onions
4½ tablespoons sugar
7 tablespoons water
oil for frying
4 cloves garlic, finely chopped

1 tablespoon fish sauce
1 tablespoon lime or lemon juice
pinch salt
1 tablespoon brown sugar
⅓ green capsicum, julienned, to garnish

Shell and devein prawns. Remove heads but retain tails. Finely chop 3 spring onions. Cut the remaining 2 into thin strips 2.5 cm long.

In a saucepan, heat sugar until golden, add 3 tablespoons of water and stir until sugar dissolves. Bring to boil, then simmer gently for about 3 minutes until caramel darkens but doesn't burn. Remove pot from heat and add remaining water. Take care caramel does not spatter. Reheat, stirring quickly to remove lumps.

Heat oil in heavy pan and fry chopped spring onion and garlic over medium heat. Add prawns for a few minutes until they are pink. Slowly pour fish sauce and warm caramel over prawn mixture in pan. Cook for 1 minute before adding lime or lemon juice, salt, brown sugar and spring onion slivers. Stir together and serve topped with capsicum strips.

Soups

Soups
Pho Goodness Sake

On a short or extended stay in Vietnam, a visitor could exist totally on soup – and yet never become bored nor fail to be tantalised.

In Vietnam, soup begins, sustains and ends each day. Pho (pronounced 'fur') is the addictive national dish based on a rich, slowly cooked, clear, beef consummé with noodles, aromatic with spices, ginger and cinnamon. Pho is secretively prepared according to family recipes by competitive sellers. These secret ingredients give pho subtle variety. Gourmets and food writers have described pho as Vietnam in a bowl of soul comfort. The name derives from the French pot au feu.

Light as consommé, but chock full of vegetables, meat or fish, with Chinese, Thai and French influences, Vietnamese soups make marvellously hearty lunches when served with crusty bread and, perhaps, a tossed green salad.

Sour fish soup is almost as much an institution as beef pho. Crab and asparagus soup features on many Vietnamese menus.

For fun at brunch, introduce chao or rice porridge to friends. It can comprise chicken, duck, fish or oysters combined with pork and at least one green vegetable. You can experiment as the Vietnamese do. Sliced red chilli, fish sauce and black pepper should be served in separate small shared bowls for diners to add to their chao at liberty.

Soups can be served in individual bowls or a large tureen for self-service at the table. Supply guests with chopsticks as well as soup spoons.

Fish With Tomato and Dill

3 medium tomatoes
750 g (24 oz) freshwater fish fillets
6 cups chicken stock
2 tablespoons fresh dill, chopped
salt and pepper
extra fresh dill

Chop tomatoes into wedges. Cut fish into large bite-sized chunks. Boil stock. Add fish, and turn down to simmer for 6 minutes. Skim surface froth and add tomatoes, dill, and salt and pepper to taste.

Simmer a little longer until fish is cooked but not breaking up. Serve in large bowl or individual bowls and garnish with fresh dill.

This chunky soup is a good starter or as part of a multi-course Vietnamese meal. It also makes a family lunch or dinner when served with fresh baguettes and a salad.

Beef Pho

250 g (9 oz) thick steak in one piece
250 g (9 oz) rice noodles
2 tablespoons fish sauce
455 g (15½ oz) flat, thick dried noodles
½ cup of bean sprouts
1 brown onion, thinly sliced
3 spring onions, finely chopped

TO SERVE
½ cup fresh coriander, torn into sprigs
½ cup Vietnamese mint leaves, chopped
1 small red chilli, seeded and sliced into rings
2 limes cut into wedges

STOCK
12 cups water
1 kg (2 lb 4 oz) shin beef bones
340 g (12 oz) gravy beef
1 large brown, unpeeled onion, halved
3 medium pieces unpeeled ginger root,
   sliced pinch of salt
1 cinnamon stick
6 whole cloves
6 peppercorns
6 coriander seeds
4 whole star anise
2 unpeeled carrots, cut into chunks

To make stock, pour water into a large pot and add shin bones and gravy beef. Bring to the boil. Skim off foaming scum from surface. Turn heat to medium-low, partly cover and simmer for 2 hours, skimming often. Add remaining stock ingredients. Simmer another 90 minutes and remove from heat.

Drain stock through a fine sieve, then set stock aside. Discard bones, carrots, onion and spices. Skim fat from stock once cool. Cut gravy beef finely across the grain. Slice steak to paper thin slices and set aside. Soak rice noodles in warm water for about 20 minutes until soft. Drain and set noodles aside.

Set stock to boil with fish sauce then reduce heat to very low. Fill a separate large pot three-quarters full of water and bring to the boil. Add dried noodles and washed bean sprouts. Continue boiling until noodles are tender but not mushy. Bean sprouts should retain some crispness. Pour boiling stock into 6 serving bowls, add drained noodles, then top equally with gravy beef, raw onion rings, chopped spring onions and raw steak slices, and garnish with coriander and mint leaves. (Diners may help themselves to chilli rings and lime wedges).

Asparagus and Crab Meat Soup

Serves 4–6

4 cups chicken broth

1 tablespoon plus 2 teaspoons fish sauce

½ teaspoon sugar

¼ teaspoon salt

1 tablespoon vegetable oil

6 shallots, chopped

2 cloves garlic, chopped

225 g (8 oz) crab meat

freshly ground black pepper

2 tablespoons cornflour or arrowroot, mixed with 2 tablespoons cold water

1 egg, lightly beaten

425 g (14½ oz) canned white asparagus spears, cut into 2.5 cm (1 in) sections, canning liquid reserved

1 tablespoon coriander leaves, shredded

1 spring onion, thinly sliced

Combine broth, 1 tablespoon of fish sauce, sugar and salt in a 3.5 litre soup pot. Bring to the boil. Reduce heat and simmer.

Meanwhile, heat oil in a skillet. Add shallots and garlic and stir-fry until aromatic. Add crab meat, the remaining 2 teaspoons of fish sauce and black pepper to taste.

Stir-fry over high heat for 1 minute. Set aside.

Bring the soup to a boil. Add cornflour mixture and stir gently until the soup thickens and is clear. While the soup is actively boiling, add egg and stir gently.

Continue to stir for about 1 minute. Add crab meat mixture and asparagus with its canning liquid. Cook gently until heated through.

Transfer the soup to a heated tureen. Sprinkle on the coriander, spring onion and freshly ground black pepper.

If white asparagus is unavailable, use frozen or fresh asparagus to the broth in step 1 and cook until tender, before adding the remaining ingredients.

Hot and Sour Fish Soup

Serves 4–6

1 kg (2 1b 4 oz) firm-fleshed fish such as
   red snapper,

1½ tablespoons nuoc cham dipping sauce

¼ teaspoon white pepper

1 spring onion, chopped

6 cups water

2 stalks lemongrass, cut into 5 cm (2 in)
   lengths and crushed lightly

55 g (2 oz) tamarind pulp

¾ cup boiling water

1 tablespoon sugar

¾ cup sliced bamboo shoots

1 cup sliced pineapple

2 tomatoes, cut into wedges

1 cup bean sprouts

mixed fresh Vietnamese herbs such as
   coriander, bitter herb, Asian basil

deep-fried shallots

lime wedges and sliced chilli to serve

Remove head, fins and tail from fish and cut into 8–10 large pieces. Combine fish, nuoc cham, pepper and spring onion, allow to marinate for 15 minutes.

Place water in a large saucepan and bring to the boil. Add the fish with its marinade and lemongrass. Reduce heat and simmer for 20 minutes.

Meanwhile, combine tamarind pulp and boiling water and allow to soak for 15 minutes. Strain mixture through a fine sieve and discard pulp.

Add the tamarind liquid, sugar, bamboo shoots, pineapple and tomatoes to the pan. Simmer for 4–5 minutes until fish is tender.

Divide bean sprouts amongst serving bowls and spoon hot soup over. Sprinkle with fresh herbs and deep-fried shallots. Serve with lime wedges and sliced chilli on the side.

CABBAGE PARCELS IN SOUP

Serves 6

24 cabbage leaves
6 spring onions
4 tablespoons coriander, finely chopped
1 cup pork, minced
½ cup prawns, minced
grated black pepper
6¼ cups chicken or pork stock
2½ tablespoons fish sauce

Blanch cabbage leaves in boiling water and cut away any tough sections from their bases.

Cut white roots from spring onions and finely chop 4 white heads. Slice 2 for garnish. Halve green stalks lengthwise to make strips.

Thoroughly mix well-chopped spring onions and 2 tablespoons of coriander with pork and prawns. Season with pepper. Set stock to boil.

Into each cabbage leaf, place 1 tablespoon of mixture. Fold the leaf base over, then the outer edges and roll up. Carefully tie up each roll with a length of green spring onion and place parcels gently into boiling stock to cook for 6 minutes.

Lift parcels into bowls, pour a cup of stock over each and garnish with remaining sliced spring onions and coriander. Dip rolls into fish sauce when eating.

DUCK AND NUT SOUP

Serves 6

400 g (14 oz) duck or chicken
peanut oil
8 cups stock or water plus 2 teaspoons salt
2 cups mixed nuts, crushed
440 g (15 oz) lychees or logan berries, drained

TO GARNISH
coriander leaves

Cut duck into bite-sized pieces. Fry in a little peanut oil until golden. Boil stock or water with salt. Add duck and simmer for 45 minutes. Skim till broth is clear.

Add nuts and simmer another 45 minutes. Add lychees or logan berries 5 minutes before serving. Garnish with coriander leaves.

Vermicelli and Chicken Soup

Serves 6

1 cup chicken breast chunks

225 g (8 oz) Chinese mung bean vermicelli

½ cup of dried wood ear mushrooms, soaked or $1/2$ cup canned button mushrooms, sliced

salt to taste

½ teaspoon black or white pepper

2 tablespoons spring onions, chopped

STOCK

8 cups water

3 teaspoons fish sauce

1 onion, quartered

1.5 kg (3lb 5 oz) pork bones

455 g (15 oz) chicken wings, bones and/or leftover meat scraps

455 g (15 oz) of 2 of the following: whole carrot, quartered cauliflower, whole green beans and/or quarter of a cabbage

Make stock by boiling all ingredients together then simmering for 1 hour. Strain reduced stock and discard the bones and vegetables.

Boil chicken chunks in stock for 15 minutes, skimming scum from the surface. Add vermicelli and soaked dried mushrooms, stalks, removed or canned mushrooms, and cook until vermicelli is done.

Season with salt and pepper and serve sprinkled with chopped spring onion.

You can use packaged stock if you prefer.

Meat

Meat
East meets west

It's amazing that pho (beef soup) sellers ladle out their addictive national dish 24 hours a day, considering meat and certainly beef, is relatively expensive in Vietnam. Family members often work in shifts around the clock to keep their pho stalls open.

Home cooks utilise beef in many ways, usually in dishes loaded with other ingredients to save on cost while still enjoying the flavour of beef. The most common meat is pork, which is both cheaper and more easily available than beef. Minced, pork is often combined with seafood to give extra texture and taste to an appetiser or main dish. All meats combine magically with fish sauce – an essential in almost every Vietnamese dish.

Vietnam's climate and terrain are unsuitable for the raising of sheep, so lamb and mutton are not included in authentic menus but can be prepared instead of beef and sometimes pork in your own kitchen. Goats roam villages and around humble countryside dwellings in Vietnam but their meat doesn't make frequent appearances in Vietnamese restaurants or at street stalls.

In Vietnam, buffalo, frog, horse, rabbit, veal and venison are also eaten. Choose cheap cuts of beef for slow pot cooking and do try caramelised pork, a southern specialty. Meat, as well as chicken liver, is often used to make Vietnamese pâté, which can serve as a luncheon dish with salad and a baguette. Meat in wrappers or skewered for barbecues is also very popular.

Some recipes in this section call for a garnish. All can be served as part of a multi-course meal but for a simple family meal, serve just one course with rice or noodles and a salad or vegetables.

Coconut Pork Stew

1 kg (2 lb 4 oz) boneless pork, cut into large cubes
4 tablespoons vegetable oil
2½ cups coconut milk
6 hard-boiled eggs
3 spring onions and ½ cup bean sprouts to garnish
nuoc cham dipping sauce
Marinade
3 cloves garlic, crushed
pinch salt
1½ tablespoons sugar
4 tablespoons fish sauce

Combine marinade ingredients and add pork, stirring so pork is completely covered. Marinate for at least 2 hours.

Heat oil in a heavy-based pan and add pork cubes, turning to sear all sides. Drain off any oil, add coconut milk and bring almost to the boil. Reduce heat, skim off surface scum and simmer, covered for about 45 minutes, until tender.

Peel hard-boiled eggs, add to pan and cook for about 10 minutes. Serve with dipping sauce and garnished with 3 spring onions cut into narrow 5 cm (2 in) strips and ½ cup of bean sprouts.

BEEF CURRY

1 kg (2 lb 4 oz) stewing beef, cubed
1 large onion, sliced
4 cloves garlic, crushed
2 tablespoons fresh ginger, crushed
2 red chillies, seeded and chopped finely
3½ tablespoons hot curry powder
2 teaspoons turmeric
1 teaspoon black ground pepper
1½ teaspoons salt
1 cup water

4½ tablespoons fish sauce
⅓ cup vegetable oil
1 tablespoons sugar
3 large carrots, chopped
3 tablespoons cornflour
2¼ cups coconut milk

TO GARNISH
coriander leaves

Combine beef, onion, garlic, ginger, chillies, curry powder, turmeric, pepper and 1 teaspoon of salt. Cover with plastic wrap and marinate in refrigerator overnight. Turn occasionally.

Heat oil in a large, heavy-based saucepan, on high heat. Add beef, turning to seal in flavours, before pouring in the water, ½ teaspoon salt and fish sauce. After boiling, cover with lid and turn down heat to simmer for about 1 hour until meat is cooked. Add sugar and carrots and cook until carrots are done (about 15 minutes).

Add cornflour to coconut milk, stirring to dissolve, and pour into curry, stirring for 10–15 minutes until curry thickens. Serve in a casserole dish with rice and salad. Garnish with coriander leaves.

Caramelised Pork

Serves 4

oil for frying
750 g (1lb 10 oz) pork, cubed
2 cloves garlic, finely chopped
2 medium onions, sliced
⅓ cup sugar
¾ cup water
1½ tablespoon fish sauce
1½ tablespoons lime juice
1 seeded red chilli, sliced and minced
½ teaspoon five spice powder
2 spring onions, chopped, to garnish

Heat oil in a heavy-based pan, add pork cubes and turn until brown. Add garlic and onion and cook, stirring to separate onion rings until transparent. Remove from heat.

To make caramel, mix sugar with water in a separate saucepan and stir over low heat until sugar dissolves. Bring to the boil then turn down to simmer, still stirring, until liquid is golden. Take pot off heat and carefully add fish sauce and lime juice. Return to heat, stirring quickly to remove any lumps, until the sauce reduces a little.

Quickly return pork, garlic and onions to reheat, add chilli and five spice and then caramel. Cook for 1 minute, stirring until combined. Transfer to serving dish and sprinkle spring onions on top.

For easier washing up, fill the pot in which the caramel has cooked with boiling water.

Sizzling Spare Ribs

8 dried mushrooms
2 spring onions
1 green capsicum
1 red chilli
500 g (17½ oz) pork or beef spare ribs
oil for deep-frying
½ teaspoon salt
½ teaspoon sugar
1 teaspoon dark soy sauce
⅓ cup water

MARINADE

½ teaspoon salt
½ teaspoon dry sherry
1 tablespoon light soy sauce
2 teaspoons cornflour

SAUCE

½ teaspoon cornflour
dash of sesame oil
ground black pepper
1½ tablespoons fish sauce

TO GARNISH

mint sprigs

Soak mushrooms for 40 minutes in hot water. Remove stalks and discard. Cut spring onions into 3.5 cm (2½ in) pieces. Seed green capsicum and chilli and cut into pieces. Combine marinade ingredients.

Chop spare ribs into large bite-sized pieces and marinate 30 minutes. Deep-fry until brown. Remove from oil. Sauté spring onions and mushrooms in a little oil, add ribs with ½ teaspoon salt, sugar, dark soy sauce and ⅓ cup water and stir-fry. Add capsicum, chilli and combined sauce ingredients.

Stir-fry, stirring, until capsicum just starts to lose crispness. Serve on a pre-heated heavy-metal grill pan so meat sizzles. Serve garnished with mint sprigs.

Vietnamese Beef

Serves 4

500 g (17½ oz) fillet steak
½ cup vegetable oil
1 cup spring onions, sliced
500 g (17½ oz) canned bamboo shoots, drained and sliced
pinch salt
1½ tablespoons fish sauce
2 cloves garlic, minced
¼ cup sesame seeds

Slice steak into thin 5 cm (2 in) strips. In a pan, heat half the oil and stir-fry beef for 1 minute, then remove from pan.

Heat remaining oil and sauté spring onions and bamboo shoots for 3 minutes. Add salt and fish sauce and cook, stirring, for 5 minutes. Add garlic and cook for a further 2 minutes.

Return steak to pan and cook until just tender. Remove from heat, add sesame seeds, stir through and serve.

Beef With Eggplant

500 g (17½ oz) eggplant, halved lengthwise
3 cloves garlic
vegetable oil
225 g (8 oz) beef mince
2 tablespoons fish sauce
salt
freshly ground black pepper

Char-grill eggplants over a barbecue or under a grill until skin blackens. Cool, peel and cut into pieces. Peel and mince garlic.

In a heavy-based pan, heat oil, then add garlic, stirring until soft. Add beef mince and cook, stirring it with a spoon until beef loses its pinkness. Add eggplant, fish sauce and salt and pepper to taste. Turn down heat to simmer. before covering. Cook and cover about 25 minutes or until eggplant has lost its firmness.

BARBECUED PORK BALLS

1 tablespoon dry sherry
1 teaspoon salt
1 teaspoon sugar
3 cloves garlic, minced
500 g (17½ oz) pork, finely minced
1½ tablespoons ground rice
1 tablespoon fish sauce
1½ tablespoons peanut oil

EQUIPMENT
bamboo skewers, pre-soaked to prevent burning

Combine sherry, salt, sugar and garlic. Add pork, combine and let stand for 2 hours.

Add ground rice, fish sauce and peanut oil, mix well then form mixture into small balls, about walnut size. Put balls on to bamboo skewers, squeezing tightly so balls adhere to skewers.

Barbecue or grill, turning often, until pork is cooked.

Beef, Cauliflower and Mushroom Stir-Fry

Serves 4

225 g (8 oz) steak, sliced into 5 cm (2 in) strips
¼ cauliflower, divided into florets
½ cup water or stock
200 g (7 oz) fresh whole button mushrooms
1½ teaspoons cornflour
2 tablespoons fish sauce
1 teaspoon oyster sauce
ground black pepper
vegetable oil
3 cloves garlic, finely chopped
1 medium onion, cut lengthwise into 8 pieces

TO GARNISH
coriander sprigs

Cut cauliflower florets in half. Mix water and mushroom liquid with cornflour, 1 tablespoon fish sauce and oyster sauce.

Pour 1 tablespoon of fish sauce over sliced meat and sprinkle pepper over. Turn meat and let stand 20 minutes.

In a pan, heat oil over high heat. Add garlic and onion and stir-fry until onion separates and softens. Add cauliflower and mushrooms. Cover, reduce heat and cook for 4 minutes. Add meat and cook until meat is cooked to your liking. Stir in cornflour mixture. Continue stirring until sauce thickens. Spoon onto a serving plate and garnish with coriander sprigs.

Baked Pork Loaf

Serves 6–8

12 dried mushrooms
8 spring onions, finely chopped
1 kg (2 lb 4 oz) minced pork
2 tablespoons fish sauce
5 eggs, beaten
pinch salt
ground black pepper

TO GARNISH
coriander leaves

In hot water, soak mushrooms for 40 minutes then squeeze out liquid, remove stems and chop mushroom tops very finely. Place mushrooms, spring onions and pork in a bowl. Add fish sauce, eggs and salt and pepper to taste and combine thoroughly.

Preheat oven to 200°C (400°F). Grease a loaf tin, then add meat mixture, patting down firmly. Cover with foil, sealing well. Sit loaf tin in a large roasting pan, pour hot water until halfway up the loaf tin and place in oven for about 1 hour or until done. Test with a knife which should come out cleanly.

Allow the loaf to cool a little, then run knife around the sides of the tin and turn out. Slice and garnish with coriander.

Sweet and Sour Meat Balls

Serves 4

225 g (8 oz) onions, finely chopped
oil for frying
225 g (8 oz) beef, minced
225 g (8 oz) pork, minced
1 egg, beaten
115 g (4 oz) rice, cooked
extra salt and pepper
1 cup plain seasoned flour

BATTER
1 egg
85 g (3 oz) flour
⅔ cup water

SWEET AND SOUR SAUCE
55 g (2 oz) onions, finely chopped
4 tablespoons dry sherry
2 tablespoons white vinegar
2 tablespoons sugar
1 cup beef stock
1 cup pineapple juice
4 teaspoons tomato purée
55 g (2 oz) pineapple, chopped
1 teaspoon fresh ginger, chopped
1 clove garlic, finely chopped
pinch chilli powder
1 tablespoon arrowroot
water

Fry onion in oil until tender. Drain and add to combination of minced meats, beaten egg and cooked rice. Mix well. Add extra salt and pepper to taste. Form mixture into small balls.

Combine batter ingredients. Gently toss balls in seasoned flour. Dip in batter and fry until golden. Drain and set aside.

For the sauce, fry onions until tender, add sherry, vinegar, sugar, stock and pineapple juice and boil 6 minutes. Add tomato purée and boil for a further 4 minutes.

Purée pineapple, ginger and garlic with a little water and add to sauce along with chilli powder. (Add more to taste if desired.) Blend arrowroot with more water until smooth and add to sauce. Stir until clear and thick, adding more water if too thick. Add meat balls to sauce to heat through before serving.

NOODLE PANCAKE WITH GARLIC BEEF

300 g (10½ oz) fillet steak

3 teaspoons minced garlic

6 tablespoons vegetable oil

½ red capsicum, seeded and cut into
slivers

½ teaspoon ground black pepper

400 g (14 oz) fresh, soft noodles

1 tablespoon sugar

1 dessertspoon fish sauce

½ cup beef stock

1 dessertspoon cornflour

2 spring onions, chopped

Serves 4 as a main course or 8 as an entrée

Part-freeze steak to make it easier to cut each piece into very thin slices. Place steak on a plate and spread with garlic, 1 tablespoon oil and capsicum. Cover and refrigerate for 45 minutes.

Pour 2½ tablespoons oil into a heavy-based pan, ensuring the base is coated. Separate the noodles with your hands. Heat oil to medium, add noodles and press them down with a spatula. Heat until base is golden and crisp. Don't lift the noodle pancake for about 15 minutes as it will break up.

Loosen edges and base of pancake gently. Place a large plate over the pan and quickly invert the pan to settle the pancake on the plate. Gently slide the pancake back into the pan, uncooked side down, and continue cooking for 5–10 minutes. Return pancake to plate in the same manner and keep warm in very slow oven.

In same pan, heat over high heat 2½ tablespoons oil. Add meat and capsicum mixture and sear quickly on both sides. Don't overcook. Mix sugar, fish sauce, stock and cornflour until smooth and add to steak. Turn meat to absorb flavours, then remove. Stir sauce rapidly until thick, returning steak briefly to coat with sauce.

Serve steak and sauce on top of pancake and cut into 4 (or 8 if presenting as an entrée). Top with sauce and garnish with chopped spring onions.

Seafood

Seafood
For a song

Seafood and fish are abundant in Vietnam with its long, curved coastline and its hinterland river systems. Visitors to Vietnam will feel that they are millionaires in Vietnam. This is not just because the currency, the dong, translates into notes confusingly worth millions, but because visitors can dine so royally on crabs, prawns, shrimp, oysters, mussels and more for a fraction of the cost than at home.

In Vietnam, fish and shellfish staples along with rice (and a great source of protein) and are inevitably the first foods to sell out at sea- and river-port markets.

Because of a general lack of refrigeration, food freshness is imperative. Therefore many markets and restaurants offer their customers live fish swimming in tanks or in plastic buckets. Its difficult to buy live fish in western countries, but you can assess freshness of your purchases by checking that the scales are not flaky and peeling, that the eyes are clear and prominent and that the gills are pink.

And, provided the fruits of the ocean and rivers are not enclosed in thick batter or drenched with rich sauces, they are delights for dieters – especially when prepared in some of the interesting ways described in the following recipes.

Rarely presented as crumbed calamari, squid is widely appreciated in Vietnam but, at home, avoid over cooking so that its texture does not become rubbery and tough. Soak it overnight in milk.

Sometimes crab can be difficult to buy fresh but crabmeat in a can substitutes well. In dishes where either prawns or shrimp need to be chopped, use either.

Vietnam has several fish not found in western waters so some recipes generalise on the type of fish required. Like the Chinese, Vietnamese are partial to carp which foreigners tend to avoid as it is so bony. However, it is a tasty fish when baked and served with a sweet and sour sauce which you'll find in this book.

Salt and Pepper Squid

500 g (17½ oz) squid, cleaned
3 tablespoons self-raising flour
1 tablespoon cornflour
1 tablespoon custard powder or 1 egg
4 tablespoons cold water
vegetable oil for deep-frying
small onion, cut into little pieces
1 clove garlic, crushed
2 tablespoons fresh parsley or
  coriander, chopped

1 teaspoon sugar
½ teaspoon salt
1½ teaspoons ground white pepper
½ teaspoon five spice powder
drops of dry sherry (optional)
parsley or coriander sprigs
nuoc cham dipping sauce

Angle-cut squid into square pieces, open up with knife and score each piece with a criss-cross. Dry squid.

Make a smooth batter of flour, cornflour and custard powder with water. If using egg instead of custard powder, add a little more flour as mixture should not be too runny.

Cover squid with batter and leave for a few minutes. Heat oil in wok or frying pan and deep-fry squid for about 3 minutes then remove squid and most of the oil. In remaining oil, place onion and garlic and cook until just tender. Add parsley or coriander and stir for 30 seconds. Return squid to pan and sprinkle with combined sugar, salt, pepper and five spice powder. Gently stir through to combine.

Toss vermicelli into hot oil for near-instant crispy noodles for the base of a serving plate. Place squid on top, sprinkle a few drops of sherry on top (optional) and garnish with parsley or coriander sprigs. Serve with nuoc cham dipping sauce.

Claypot Fish

1 tablespoon vegetable oil
370 g (13 oz) freshwater fish, cut into bite-sized pieces
115 g (4 oz) pork loin, sliced
10 cloves garlic, finely chopped
1 cup chicken stock
½ cup sugar
2 chillies, seeded and finely chopped
1 medium onion, sliced
1 tablespoon fish sauce
1 medium-sized tomato, sliced

Heat oil in a pan. Add fish, and fry lightly until just brown. Transfer fish to a clay pot or stove-top casserole. Brown pork in pan and add to fish along with garlic, stock, sugar and chilli. Stir to combine. Cover and cook on medium heat until sauce is thickened.

In pan, sauté onion slices until tender. Add fish sauce to pot and cook, stirring. When cooked, place onions on top of pork and fish. Place fresh tomato on top just before serving.

Prawn Curry

2 tablespoons vegetable oil
2 cloves garlic, finely chopped
12 king prawns, cooked
1 onion, sliced
1 medium zucchini, sliced
½ green capsicum, seeded and sliced
½ tablespoon green curry paste
1 cup coconut milk
1 teaspoon cornflour
1 tablespoon water
1 teaspoon sugar
1 tablespoon fish sauce

TO SERVE
coriander leaves and steam rice

Heat oil in pan. Add garlic and prawns and stir-fry for 2 minutes. Add onion, zucchini and capsicum, stirring for 2 more minutes. Remove from stove.

In another pan, place curry paste and stir constantly for 1 minute. Add coconut milk and bring to the boil. Mix cornflour with water and add sugar, fish sauce and prawns with vegetables. Garnish with coriander leaves and serve with steamed rice.

CHILLI CRAB WITH LEMONGRASS

Serves 2–4

1 large crab (1.3 kg/ 3 lb)) or 2 smaller
  crabs
1 tablespoon oil
2 cloves garlic, finely chopped
1 onion, sliced
1 stalk lemongrass, finely sliced
4 chillies, sliced
2 tablespoons fish sauce
2 tablespoons lime juice

½ cup water
4 spring onions, cut into 2.5 cm (1 in)
  pieces
½ cup bean shoots and
  deep-fried shallots, to garnish
extra lime juice and nuoc cham dipping
  sauce to serve

Clean the crab well. Heat oil in a large saucepan, stir-fry garlic, onion, lemongrass and chilli over high heat for a few minutes.

Pour fish sauce, lime juice and water into the pan and bring to the boil. Carefully place crab in saucepan. Cover with a tightly fitting lid. Cook over a medium high heat for 10–15 minutes until the crab is cooked.

Place crab on a serving platter. Add spring onions to the pan, heat cooking liquid until reduced to about ¼ cup and pour over the crab.

Arrange bean shoots over the hot crab, sprinkle liberally with deep-fried shallots and serve with extra lime juice and dipping sauce.

Barbecued prawns

500 g (17½ oz) large green prawns
170 g (6 oz) thin rice vermicelli
boiling water
2 teaspoons vegetable oil
6 spring onions, chopped
½ cup roasted peanuts
½ bunch coriander leaves, chopped
nuoc cham dipping sauce

Slit prawns down back, remove vein, wash and pat dry. Cook prawns over charcoal or on barbecue for about 5 minutes, turning once.

Add vermicelli to boiling water and boil for 2 minutes. Drain and rinse under cold running water.

Heat oil in wok or frying pan, add spring onions and fry until softened. Arrange spring onions and vermicelli on warmed serving plates, top with prawns, then sprinkle with shallots and peanuts. Pour hot nuoc cham over top and sprinkle with coriander.

Nha Trang Eel

1½ tablespoons peanut oil

1 tablespoon ginger root, finely chopped

1 tablespoon garlic, finely chopped

2 tablespoons spring onions, finely
chopped

500 g (17½ oz) scallops, including corals

SAUCE

1 tablespoon rice wine or dry sherry

2 teaspoons light soy sauce

2 teaspoons dark soy sauce

2 tablespoons chilli bean sauce

2 teaspoons tomato paste

1 teaspoon sugar

½ teaspoon salt

½ teaspoon sugar

2 teaspoons sesame oil

Serves 4–6

Wash eel, skin it, remove backbone and cut into bite-sized pieces. Soak mushrooms in boiling water for 30 minutes then remove and discard stems. Cut capsicum into 2.5·cm (1 in) squares. Drain pineapple, reserving ½ cup of the canning juice.

Heat 1 tablespoon oil in pan over medium heat and fry garlic and onions until soft. Add eel, capsicum, fish sauce and a sprinkle of pepper to taste. Stir-fry until eel has softened, adding more oil if necessary. Add pineapple pieces, tomatoes and mushrooms, stirring to heat through.

Combine cornflour with pineapple juice and add to pan. Serve once sauce was thickened, garnished with parsley.

CRAB MEAT BOATS

Serves 6 as an appetiser, or 3 as a main course.

3 eggplants
3 spring onions, chopped
oil for cooking
1½ cups crabmeat, cooked or canned
coriander sprigs to garnish

SAUCE

2 small, red chillies, seeded and minced
2 tablespoons peanuts, crushed
¼ cup fish sauce
1 teaspoon sugar
3 tablespoons water

Halve eggplants lengthwise and brush with oil. Barbecue or grill, turning frequently until flesh softens completely and skin darkens. Carefully peel off skins and discard but retain split stem for decorative purpose. Keep eggplant boats warm in oven.

Fry two-thirds of spring onions in oil until golden. Add sauce ingredients, cook until sugar is dissolved then add crab meat and heat through.

Place eggplant boats on one large or individual plates. Spoon over equal amounts of crab meat and sauce and garnish with remaining chopped spring onion and coriander sprigs.

Cooked, chopped or small, whole prawns can substituted for crab meat if desired.

Hanoi-Style Fried Fish

salt and pepper
¼ cup peanut oil
4 teaspoons turmeric, grated
1 heaped teaspoon ginger, grated
4 spring onions, chopped
½ cup fresh dill, chopped
2 tablespoons crushed peanuts

DIPPING SAUCE

2 tablespoons shrimp paste with soya bean oil
¼ cup fish sauce
1 tablespoon sugar
500 g (17½ oz) boneless fish fillets

TO GARNISH

lettuce and mint leaves

Prepare dipping sauce by mixing shrimp paste, a little extra oil, fish sauce and sugar.
Boil and add more sugar if desired.

Season fish with salt and pepper and cut into 2.5 cm (1in) pieces. In a heavy-based
pan, heat oil, then add fish, turmeric and ginger. Turn gently and just before fish is
done, add spring onions, dill and peanuts. Serve with dipping sauce, lettuce and mint
on a bed of rice.

Squid Cakes

2 tablespoons pork fat, finely chopped
1 dessertspoon dry sherry
pinch salt
1 teaspoon sugar
2 teaspoons ground pepper
1 small seeded orange chilli seeded
    and finely chopped
500 g (17½ oz) squid, finely chopped
2 tablespoons parsley, chopped
3 spring onions, chopped
3 teaspoons fish sauce
1 egg
vegetable oil

SAUCE

2 teaspoons fish sauce
2 teaspoons lime or lemon juice or vinegar
2 teaspoons sugar
3 teaspoons water

TO GARNISH

1 lime
½ red capsicum, seeded
½ cucumber
coriander sprigs

Boil pork fat to soften then finely chop again. Add sherry, salt, sugar and pepper. Set aside.

Meanwhile, reserve a pinch of chopped chilli for sauce. Add the remainder to squid with parsley and spring onions. Put fish sauce in wok and heat until wok is nearly dry (to flavour it) and add any crystals to squid.

Separate egg and lightly beat white and yolk in individual bowls. Combine pork fat mixture with squid and add enough egg white to bind. Oil your hands and make flat cakes of squid. Lightly fry in wok or frypan, turning in oil, adding more oil as necessary. Cakes will expand. Remove squid cakes and allow to cool. Wipe wok or pan clean with kitchen paper. Dip cakes in egg yolk to give yellow colour and re-fry in more fresh oil.

Combine sauce ingredients with reserved chilli. Slowly heat until sugar is dissolved.

Thinly slice lime and capsicum. Halve lime rings and arrange in a circle on a plate with thin slices of cucumber. Add hot squid cakes, serve with a bowl of sauce on the side and garnish with coriander sprigs.

Chicken and Poultry

Chicken and Poultry
Out for a duck

One has only to stroll through a market in Hanoi, Saigon or one of hundreds of villages and towns in Vietnam to realise how popular poultry is with the Vietnamese.

Strung up in busy meat sections, plump, live and feathered in wicker cages, chicken is favoured over red meat for its versatility and economy.

In some of Vietnam's most picturesque regions, where strangely shaped rocky outcrops dominate rice paddies, ducks are farmed, forming noisy, moving foregrounds against stunning scenery. Ducks are revered in the kitchen for their adaptability. While meat, poultry and fish are not eaten in households every day, duck and chicken are the most favoured meats in Vietnam next to pork.

Almost every part of the bird is used, even its feet which, some believe, uplift the spirit. Chicken and duck feet are popular with young women who eat them when they want to pamper themselves.

The Greeks regard bull testicles as a delicacy that encourages virility. Vietnam has a similar philosophy about rooster testicles. The proud, strutting rooster's genitalia are tasty, but not included in our recipes. If they're available and you're intrigued, sauté rooster testes and serve with a sweet and sour sauce with diced ham and peas added.

In salads, roasts, grills, stir-fries, slow cook pots, fricassees, curries and appetisers, poultry makes frequent appearances and can replace seafood if diners are allergic to shellfish.

Indeed, most dishes using seafood in this book are amenable to preparation with chicken instead. Some recipes the influence of former occupying and neighbouring countries.

For cutting up poultry Asian-style, a sharp cleaver is indispensable.

Stir-Fried Lemongrass Chicken

Serves 4

4 stalks lemongrass
500 g (17½ oz) skinless boneless chicken breasts, cut into 2.5 cm (1 in) cubes
1 teaspoon sesame oil
2 tablespoons vegetable oil
1 red capsicum, deseeded and chopped
2 tablespoons roasted salted peanuts, roughly chopped
1 tablespoon fish sauce
1 tablespoon soy sauce
½ tablespoon sugar
salt
2 spring onions, chopped, to garnish

Peel the outer layers from lemongrass stalks and finely chop the lower white bulbous parts, discarding the fibrous tops. Put chicken into a large bowl, add lemongrass and sesame oil and turn to coat. Cover and marinate in the fridge for 2 hours, or overnight.

Heat a wok or large, heavy-based frying pan, and add vegetable oil. Add chicken with its marinade and stir-fry for 5 minutes or until the chicken has turned white.

Add capsicum, peanuts, fish sauce, soy sauce, sugar and salt to taste. Stir-fry for another 5 minutes or until chicken and pepper are cooked. Sprinkle with the spring onions just before serving.

Spicy Orange Duck

Serves 6

2 kg (4lb 6 oz) duck pieces
vegetable oil
3 tablespoons sugar
2 cups orange juice
2 oranges
finely sliced orange rind
2 small red chillies, seeded and sliced

MARINADE
3 tablespoons fish sauce
1 tablespoon peeled ginger root,
  finely chopped
1 tablespoon red chilli,
  seeded and finely chopped
salt and pepper
1 tablespoon vegetable oil

Combine marinade ingredients, coat both sides of duck pieces and marinate, preferably overnight.

Heat oil in pan, add duck pieces along with marinade and fry until golden. Turn pieces. Turn heat down a little. When duck is almost cooked, sprinkle half the sugar over. When time to turn again, sprinkle with rest of sugar. While sugar is becoming caramel, add orange juice, stir and remove duck pieces.

Peel oranges, cut into segments and arrange on serving plate. Add duck. Stir orange sauce until it reaches desired thickness. Pour sauce over duck pieces and decorate with pared orange rind and extra chillies.

Chicken With Cauliflower

2 large chicken fillets

2 cloves garlic, minced

salt and ground black pepper to taste

4 tablespoons vegetable oil

2 large onions, each cut into 8

2 cups small cauliflower florets

1 red chilli, seeded and chopped

SAUCE

2 tablespoons cornflour

1 dessertspoon soy sauce

1 tablespoon vinegar

1 tablespoon fish sauce

1 cup chicken stock

   (make from powder or cube will do)

Between 2 sheets of plastic film, pound chicken until thin. Slice chicken into thin strips to make almost 2 cups. Season with garlic, salt and plenty of pepper. Stir and set aside for 10 minutes.

Heat pan, add 2 tablespoons oil and sauté chicken quickly. Remove from pan. Reheat pan, add remaining oil and sauté onion until brown but not cooked. Add cauliflower florets and chilli and sauté for a further 10–15 minutes.

Mix cornflour with vinegar and sauces until smooth. Add to cup of stock.

Combine chicken with vegetables, add sauce and stir as the mixture thickens. Serve with steamed rice or noodles.

Thin rare beef strips can replace chicken.

Honey Roasted Duck

Serves 6–8

3 teaspoons ground black pepper

3 teaspoons salt

3 tablespoons sugar

2½ tablespoons peanut oil

1 medium to large whole duck

6 tablespoons honey

6 tablespoons light soy sauce

2 tablespoons lime or lemon juice

pinch saffron or turmeric (optional)

TO GARNISH

tomatoes, thinly sliced

cucumber, thinly sliced

1 red chilli, seeded and sliced

coriander

Combine together pepper, salt, sugar and 4 teaspoons of oil. Rub duck inside and out and seal flavours inside by securing the opening with a bamboo skewer. Preheat oven to 190°C (375°F).

Mix honey, soy sauce, lime or lemon juice, remaining 2 teaspoons of oil and optional saffron or turmeric used for its colour rather than flavour. Pour over duck, ensuring it reaches the whole surface (a must). Place duck in oven and baste every 20 minute until golden and cooked through (about 2 hrs).

Cut up into serving pieces, and garnish with tomatoes, cucumber, chilli and coriander sprigs.

Chicken, quails, goat and rabbit or other game may replace duck.

Spicy Chicken Skewers

1 kg (2lb 4 oz) boneless chicken fillets

1 tablespoon coconut milk

1½ teaspoons five spice powder

MARINADE

2 spring onions, chopped

1 stalk lemongrass, peeled and finely
  sliced

2½ tablespoons sugar

1 small, red chilli, seeded and crushed

1 tablespoon fish sauce

1 tablespoon soy sauce

1 tablespoon peanut oil

TO SERVE

nuoc cham dipping sauce

 peanut sauce

EQUIPMENT

bamboo skewers

Soak about 25 bamboo skewers in water overnight or in boiling water for at least 45 minutes so they will not burn when cooking. Combine marinade ingredients.

Cut chicken into thin strips, add to marinade, ensuring each strip is covered. Cover and refrigerate several hours or overnight.

Drain chicken and discard marinade. Thread chicken strips on to skewers. Barbecue or grill for about 3 minutes until brown.

Serve as part of a main course or as an appetiser with nuoc cham dipping sauce or peanut sauce.

Turkey With Mushrooms

Serves 6

1 cup dried mushrooms
1.5 kg (3 lb 5 oz) turkey hindquarter
2½ teaspoons vegetable oil
2 tablespoons soy sauce
2 tablespoons dry sherry
3 teaspoons sugar
peel from 1½ oranges
salt and pepper, to taste

TO GARNISH
mint sprigs

Soak mushrooms in boiling water for 30 minutes. Drain and discard stems. Slice.

Chop turkey hindquarter into chunks, using a cleaver to get through the bone. Pour boiling water over pieces to fatten skin then drain and dry with kitchen paper. Brown turkey, over a medium heat, in just enough oil to cover a heavy-based pan. Cook in batches, wiping pan clean with kitchen paper after each batch and adding more oil as necessary.

To a clean pan add fresh oil and return turkey along with soy sauce, sherry, sugar, mushrooms and peel from 1 orange. Bring to the boil.

Turn heat down to simmer, cover and cook, stirring and skimming scum from surface occasionally, until turkey is tender. Season with salt and pepper, remove from heat and stand covered for 5 minutes. Discard orange peel and serve topped with sauce. Garnish with pared peel from remaining ½ orange, and mint sprigs.

Chicken or duck can be used in this recipe.

CHICKEN EGG CAKES

55 g (2 oz) cellophane noodles
4 dried mushrooms
2 cloves garlic, minced
1 tablespoon vegetable oil
6 eggs
400 g (14 oz) chicken fillet, minced
1½ teaspoons sugar
2 teaspoons fresh coriander, finely
    chopped

pinch salt
ground black pepper

TO GARNISH
1 spring onion, sliced
6 sprigs coriander
nuoc cham dipping sauce
soy sauce

Soak noodles in boiling water for 10 minutes. Chop into 2 cm (1 in) sections. Soak mushrooms in boiling water for 10 minutes, drain and slice. Soften garlic in oil over medium heat. Preheat oven to 150°C (300°F).

In a bowl, beat eggs and add garlic, chicken, noodles, mushrooms, sugar, coriander and salt and pepper to taste. Combine thoroughly and pour into lightly greased heatproof soup bowls or one large bowl.

Place bowls in a baking dish and fill dish to halfway with water. Cover bowls and steam in oven (for 10–15 minutes) or until cakes are set. Remove lids for just long enough for top turn golden. Garnish with spring onions and a sprig of coriander. Serve with separate bowls of dipping sauce and soy sauce.

Minced pork, beef, prawns or crabmeat can be used instead of chicken.

Vegetables

Vegetables
Fresh, fried, cooked in a pickle

Where rice paddies do not carpet the Vietnam landscape, and no animals graze, vegetables are grown. Vegetable crops are mixed on farms and also in the countryside, where most small dwellings have little gardens. But, as many city Vietnamese inhabit apartments or sparse rooms without space to garden, and poverty is widespread, vegetables from the market are more popular even than meat. Markets offer a great choice of vegetables which are selected carefully as the Vietnamese are particular about freshness.

The lack of refrigeration in rural areas often means market shopping is done twice daily by the home cook. Block ice is still sold by some vendors but it's usually sold by the bucketful to be shaved to cool beer.

Metropolitan Asian markets or stores in western countries usually have good selections of dried, canned and packaged vegetable ingredients if vegetables are unavailable fresh.

Chillies, pineapples, tomatoes, asparagus and avocados were introduced to Vietnam over the centuries and are still popular. Preserved vegetables are sold in small containers in Asian food stores and markets but are used sparingly to flavour rice or noodles or to add flavours to soups and stews. The taste is piquant and biting.

Tofu or beancurd, made from soy beans, is widely used. Vegans visiting Vietnam will never go hungry but will need to check that fish or oyster sauce or shrimp paste has not been used in the preparation of a vegetable dish.

Spinach With Peanut Sauce

750 g (1lb 10oz) water spinach or mature spinach
3 spring onions, sliced
2 cloves garlic, crushed
1½ tablespoons vegetable oil
¼ cup peanuts, crushed
salt and pepper

PEANUT SAUCE
⅓ cup smooth peanut butter
½ cup coconut milk
1½ tablespoons sugar
⅓ cup sweet chilli sauce
2 teaspoons lime or lemon juice
⅓ cup vegetable stock

TO GARNISH
coriander sprigs

Trim stalks of water spinach. Blanch spinach in boiling water to make it limp then place in cool or iced water. Drain completely.

Make peanut sauce in saucepan by combining all ingredients and stirring over low heat until smooth.

Fry spring onions and garlic in oil until tender. Add peanuts and then spinach and peanut sauce. Season with salt and pepper and garnish with coriander sprigs.

Potato Patties

Serves 4 as an accompaniment to a main course

2 large old potatoes, peeled
pinch salt
¼ cup cornflour
1 large egg
3 spring onions, chopped
1 small onion, minced
3 cloves garlic, minced
2 teaspoons fish sauce
2 teaspoons curry powder
ground black pepper
⅔ cup vegetable oil

TO SERVE
nuoc cham dipping sauce

Grate potato or shred in a food processor. Put in a colander, sprinkle with salt and mix through. Let stand 20 minutes then squeeze out natural liquid. Place in a bowl and combine with cornflour.

Beat egg lightly and add it to potato along with remaining ingredients, except the oil. Combine well. Heat oil in a large heavy-based pan. Ladle in potato mixture by the tablespoon. Patties should be about 6 cm (2½ in) diameter.

Fry until golden (about 4 minutes) turn, and when each patty is crisp, drain on kitchen paper. Serve hot with nuoc cham dipping sauce.

Taro roots or sweet potatoes can be substituted for potatoes.

CURRIED VEGETABLES

2 stalks lemongrass

255 g (9 oz)new potatoes, peeled and
   quartered

115 g (4 oz) green beans

115 g (4 oz) carrots

1 eggplant

salt

2½ tablespoons vegetable oil

2 spring onions, thinly sliced

3 cloves garlic, crushed

3 tablespoons curry powder

2 teaspoons shrimp paste (optional)

2 dried red chillies, chopped

1 cup vegetable stock

1 cup coconut milk

1 tablespoon fish sauce

2 lime leaves or strips of lime or lemon
   peel

Prepare potatoes. Remove outer leaves and trim ends and tough tops of lemongrass. Slice as finely as possible. Trim beans. Peel carrots and cut both diagonally into 3.5 cm (2 in) pieces. Slice eggplant into 2.5 cm (1 in) rounds, salt and let stand 10 minutes then drain liquid and quarter each round.

Heat oil in a heavy-based pan, add spring onions and garlic and sauté until just golden. Add curry powder, shrimp paste if desired, lemongrass and chilli and cook about 6 minutes. Add stock, coconut milk, fish sauce and lime leaves or citrus peel. Cover and bring to the boil.

Reduce heat to medium, add carrots, potatoes, beans and eggplant. Part-cover and simmer until vegetables are tender and liquid has reduced. Season with salt.

Steamed Stuffed Cucumbers

Serves 4–6

4 dried black mushrooms
500 g (17½ oz) cucumber
1½ teaspoons cornflour
375 g (13 oz)canned water chestnuts
2½ tablespoons glutinous rice flour
sesame oil
½ teaspoon sugar
½ teaspoon salt
4 tablespoons cooked, diced carrot
vegetable oil
pepper
¾ cup stock or water

Soak mushrooms for 30 minutes, drain then remove and discard stalks, and chop the remainder.

Peel cucumbers and cut into 1 cm (½ in) pieces. Scrape seeds out and discard. Parboil cucumber shells for 1 minute. Rinse in cold water, drain and dust inside with a little cornflour.

Drain water chestnuts and discard liquid.

Mash and add rice flour, a dash of sesame oil and ¼ teaspoon each of sugar and salt. Add carrot and mushrooms and mix well. Stuff cucumber circles and place on a plate. Steam in steamer, covered, for 15 minutes.

In a separate saucepan, mix a dash of oil with pepper to taste and remaining sugar and salt. Add remaining cornflour. Stir in stock or water until smooth. Heat until thickened and pour over the cooked cucumber pieces.

HERBED RICE NOODLES WITH ASPARAGUS AND PEANUTS

Serves 4

3 tablespoons rice vinegar

1 tablespoon sugar

1 small Spanish onion, finely sliced

255 g (9 oz) dried rice noodles

2 bunches of asparagus

⅓ cup chopped fresh mint

⅓ cup chopped fresh coriander leaves

1 continental cucumber, peeled,
   seeded and thinly sliced

6 spring onions, finely sliced

3 Roma tomatoes, finely diced

¾ cup roasted peanuts, lightly crushed

juice of 2 limes

2 teaspoons fish sauce

2 teaspoons olive oil

½ teaspoon chilli flakes

Whisk rice vinegar and sugar together and pour over the finely sliced onion rings. Allow to marinate for 1 hour, tossing frequently.

Cook noodles according to packet directions. (Usually, rice noodles need only to soak in boiling water for 5 minutes, otherwise, boil for 1–2 minutes then drain immediately and rinse under cold water.)

Cut off the tough stalks of the asparagus, and cut remaining stalks into 2 cm (1 in) lengths. Simmer asparagus in salted water for 2 minutes until bright green and crisply tender. Rinse in cold water to refresh.

Toss noodles with reserved onion and vinegar mixture while still warm. Then, using kitchen scissors, cut noodles into manageable lengths (10 cm/4 in).

Add the cooked asparagus to noodles along with chopped mint, coriander, cucumber, spring onions, tomatoes and roasted peanuts and toss thoroughly.

Whisk lime juice, fish sauce, oil and chilli flakes together and drizzle over the noodle salad. Serve at room temperature.

TOFU-STUFFED TOMATOES

Serves 6

6 large, firm tomatoes
125 g (4 oz) firm tofu, drained
1 cup fresh mushrooms, chopped
3 cloves garlic, minced
4 spring onions, chopped
1 tablespoon fish sauce
1 teaspoon ground white pepper
1 egg, beaten
1 tablespoon cornflour
¼ cup vegetable oil

TO GARNISH
¼ cup coriander leaves, chopped

Cut tops from tomatoes, remove both core and pulp, and set aside. Mash tofu and mix in a bowl with mushrooms, garlic, spring onions, fish sauce, pepper, egg and cornflour. Fill tomatoes with the mixture.

Heat oil in a large frying pan over high heat then carefully add tomatoes, stuffed side down. Cook for about 4 minutes, turn to low and cook for another 6 minutes.

Serve garnished with coriander and with sweet and sour sauce.

STICKY RICE WITH BEAN SPROUTS

Serves 6

255 g (9 oz) glutinous rice
water
225 g (9 oz) fresh bean sprouts or mung dhal
pinch salt

Cover rice with water. If not using fresh bean sprouts, soak mung dhal in water in a separate bowl. Leave both to soak overnight then wash rice and mung dhal until water runs clear. Mix rice and mung dhal with salt.

   Line a bamboo steamer or top of a metal steamer with a tea towel, or greaseproof paper and spread rice and mung dhal over it. Cover with folded sides of tea towel and/or lid. Steam for about 40 minutes, replenishing water, until cooked. If using fresh bean sprouts, add to cooked rice and fluff through with a fork.

For plain sticky rice, steam as above (without bean sprouts) or boil 4 cups of water with 2 cups of soaked glutinous rice for 10 minutes. Remove from heat, drain, cover and stand for 15 minutes.

Salads

Salads
Ripe for experiments

Vietnamese salads differ from many in the world in that they often include seafoods or meats. This means that the salads can make light, nutritious main courses when served with crusty bread, so refreshing in summer. In Vietnam, salads come as part of a multi-course meal but visitors to Vietnam should check whether the raw ingredients have been washed in bottled water.

With its range of tropical and cool-climate fruits, herbs and vegetables Vietnam's colourful salads reflect different flavours and textures and are ripe for experimentation if certain ingredients are unavailable. If a daikon (large white radish) can't be found for this recipe, use red-skinned radish.

Vegetarians can omit meats and certain sauces from the following salads. Some of the dressings described in this section can be used to add exciting new flavours to familiar salad favourites.

SAIGON SALAD

8 cooked potatoes
400 g (14 oz) canned artichoke hearts
400 g (14 oz)canned button mushrooms

DRESSING

4 tablespoons white vinegar
juice of ½ lemon
¼ cup parsley, chopped
large pinch dried dill
salt to taste
ground black pepper

TO GARNISH

parsley sprigs and walnuts, quartered

Peel potatoes, slice and place in salad bowl. Combine dressing ingredients well and pour over potatoes.

Drain artichokes and mushrooms and discard liquid. Carefully mix with potatoes and dressing and garnish with parsley and walnuts.

Green Papaya Salad

750 g (1lb 1oz) green papaya, finely
  julienned
4 spring onions, very finely julienned
half daikon radish, very finely julienned
12 Vietnamese mint leaves
12 Thai basil (or regular basil) leaves
¼ bunch fresh coriander, leaves only
1 clove garlic, minced

DRESSING
¼ teaspoon shrimp paste
2 tablespoons boiling water

3 tablespoons rice vinegar
3 tablespoons lime juice
2 tablespoons fish sauce
2 tablespoons sugar
1 tablespoon sweet chilli sauce

TO GARNISH
2 tablespoons dried shrimp or crushed
  peanuts
extra Thai basil and Vietnamese mint
  leaves

Toss papaya with spring onions, radish, chopped fresh herbs and garlic.

To make the dressing, dilute shrimp paste in boiling water, then whisk with all other dressing ingredients. If the sauce is a little too acidic, add a little extra water to dilute the flavour to your taste. Continue whisking until the dressing is well mixed.

Toss dressing through papaya and vegetable mixture, taking care to disperse the dressing thoroughly.

Pile onto a plate and sprinkle with peanuts or dried shrimp. garnish with extra basil and mint leaves.

Chicken Salad

1 onion, finely sliced
1 carrot, julienned
1 radish, finely sliced
1 stick celery, finely sliced
½ green or red capsicum,
  seeded and finely sliced
2 cups cooked chicken, chopped
1 cup lettuce leaves, torn
¼ quarter cucumber, sliced diagonally

DRESSING
5 tablespoons lemon juice
⅓ cup water
3 tablespoons sugar

TO GARNISH
1 tablespoon mint, chopped
1 small red chilli, seeded and sliced

Mix dressing ingredients. Combine salad vegetables except lettuce and cucumber in a bowl. Pour over dressing, cover and refrigerate for 1 hour. Transfer to a salad bowl.

Add chicken, lettuce and cucumber, toss together and sprinkle with mint and chilli rings.

Desserts

Desserts

Vietnamese dessert, following a family home meal, is inevitably fruit. Vietnam is blessed with so many varieties of fruit, including bananas, watermelon, mangosteen, jackfruit, mango, guava, pineapple, pomelo (like grapefruit), rambutan, custard apple, lychees, tamarind, durian and more. Readers in tropical regions will have little difficulty in obtaining most of these fruits.

The French made a big impact on the creation of desserts in Vietnam. Sweetmeats, including green mung bean cakes, cookies and desserts are delicious snacks, bought between meals from hawkers, market stalls and French-style patisseries.

The Vietnamese have adapted many French dessert recipes in several ways. One adaption is to replace milk and cream with respectively, coconut milk and cream. These ingredients add a refreshing flavour and are essentially lower in cholesterol and kilojoules than the dairy equivalents. Some desserts, such as the crème caramel to follow, are called flans although no pastry is evident. Dessert soups are also unusual for westerners, but very cooling in summer. If, in Vietnam, a host offers you 'cake' (or banh), don't necessarily expect a rich gateau – although you may get it. The term 'cake' covers all sorts of sweet and savoury treats, from vegetable rolls and seafood rice crêpes to fruity tarts.

Although the habit in Vietnam is to serve all lunch and dinner dishes together around the rice pot, without dessert, you can break tradition with a triumphantly sweet finale to your own Vietnamese dinner party.

Ginger Biscuits

Makes about 20 biscuits

½ cup plain flour
½ cup caster sugar
¼ teaspoon bicarbonate of soda
pinch salt
2 tablespoons ground ginger
1 teaspoon ground cinnamon
55 g (2 oz) butter
1 tablespoon golden syrup
1 small egg

Preheat oven to 170°C (340°F). Sift flour, sugar, bicarbonate of soda and salt into a bowl.
Add ginger and cinnamon. Work butter in with hands until texture of breadcrumbs.
Beat golden syrup and egg together and gradually add to flour mix to form dough.
   Form into small balls and place well apart on to greased baking trays. Bake until crisply golden.

Coconut Flan With Caramel (Creme Caramel)

CARAMEL
¼ cup sugar
¼ cup hot water

CUSTARD
4 eggs
1 teaspoon vanilla essence

1 cup canned or reconstituted
   powdered coconut milk
1 cup milk
¼ cup sugar
mint sprig to decorate

Serves 6

To make caramel melt sugar alone in a small, heavy pot, over a low heat. Swirl the pot constantly until the sugar becomes golden. Stir in hot water carefully as the mixture will splatter. Quickly stir to dissolve any lumps and boil for about 2 minutes until liquid is clear. Pour caramel into a 4 cup soufflé dish which has been lightly greased with butter or margarine. Tilt the dish to ensure caramel coats the base.

To make custard, beat eggs and vanilla in a large bowl. Combine coconut milk and milk with sugar in a saucepan and cook over low heat until sugar dissolves. Remove from stove and beat quickly into eggs and vanilla so eggs do not curdle. Sieve custard only if it is lumpy. Pour slowly on top of caramel in soufflé dish.

Preheat oven to 160°C (320°F). In the base of a large roasting pan, place 2 layers of paper towelling, then place the soufflé dish on top before pouring hot water into the roasting pan until halfway up the soufflé dish. Bake in the centre of the oven for about 50 minutes or until a knife inserted into custard is clean when removed. Do not allow water to boil. Remove soufflé dish. Cool in a pan of cold water. Refrigerate, covered with plastic wrap, preferably overnight.

To serve, run a knife around the circumference of the dish and place a dinner plate on top. In a quick movement, invert the dish and the créme caramel will slide onto the plate. Serve alone or with whipped cream. Place a mint sprig in the centre to garnish.

Mango Cake With Nutmeg Cream

1 cup unsalted roasted macadamia nuts

3 large mangoes, about 750 g (1lb 10oz)

255 g (9 oz) butter, softened

1 teaspoon vanilla essence

1 cup caster sugar

4 large eggs

2 cups plain flour

1½ teaspoons baking powder

½ cup roasted macadamia nuts, chopped

icing sugar

2 cups pure cream

1 teaspoon nutmeg

1 mango, sliced, for serving

Preheat the oven to 180°C (360°F) and grease a 22 cm (9 in) non-stick cake tin with butter.

Crush roasted macadamia nuts in a food processor and set aside.

Peel mangoes and dice the flesh, saving as much juice as possible, then reserve some nice pieces of mango (about 85 g) and purée the remaining mango flesh with all the reserved juice. You should have about 1 cup of mango purée.

Beat softened butter and vanilla essence with half the sugar. Beat until thick and pale. While beating, add remaining sugar and beat until all sugar has been added. Add eggs, one at a time, and beat well after each addition.

In a separate bowl, combine crushed nuts, flour and baking powder.

Remove the bowl from the mixer and add the flour mixture, stirring well to combine. Add the mango purée and mix gently.

Spoon the batter into the prepared tin, then sprinkle chopped macadamia nuts and reserved diced mango over the batter and swirl through.

Bake for 1 hour, then remove the cake from the oven and cool in the tin. When cool, remove from the tin and dust with icing sugar.

To prepare the cream, whip cream and nutmeg together until the cream is thick and fragrant. Serve alongside the cake with some mango slices.

Almond Rice Jelly

85 g (3 oz) ground rice
170 g (6 oz) ground almonds
55 g (2 oz) powdered gelatine
170 g (6 oz) caster sugar
55 g (2 oz) desiccated coconut
4½ cups boiling water
few drops of almond essence

Mix together all dried ingredients in a saucepan. Add boiling water while stirring and bring to the boil. Simmer, still stirring, for 10 minutes until thick. Stir in almond essence. Pour into lightly greased serving bowl or mould, cool, cover and refrigerate.

Serve with a bowl of canned lychees, gooseberries or fresh guava and cream if desired.

Ginger Melon Soup

1 rock melon (about 750 g/ 1 lb 10 oz)
55 g (2 oz) fresh ginger, peeled
3½ cups water
100 g (3½ oz) sugar
315 g (11 oz) glass noodles
juice of 2 limes or lemons

Peel melon, remove seeds, cut into small cubes and machine-blend. Keep cool. Slice ginger finely and boil half of it in water with half the sugar until sugar has dissolved. Turn heat down, and add noodles to simmer for 5 minutes. Remove from heat, allow to cool, pour into a bowl, and remove ginger and chill.

In a saucepan, boil together remaining sugar, ginger and lime or lemon juice. Simmer until thick. Remove from heat, cool and remove ginger. Chill.

In individual bowls set in larger ice-filled bowls, pour equal quantities of gingered melon purée. Top with noodles then lime or lemon mix. Garnish each with a mint leaf and serve with ginger biscuits (see page 173) to dunk and soften.

Index

About the Author

Emily Nguyen has travelled extensively around Southeast Asia and works as a chef and food photographer. She lives with her husband and daughter in a small seaside town. This is her first book for New Holland.